The Workboot Serie
WOOL

Hey Blunnie! What do you get when you cross a kangaroo and a sheep?

A woolly jumper!

Written by Fiona Hamilton
Illustrated by Brad Holland
Published by the Kondinin Group

3

Contents

Have you ever wondered what it's really like looking after the sheep that produce all that wool for jumpers? This book will help you to find out about sheep farming in Australia and how it affects both you and our environment.

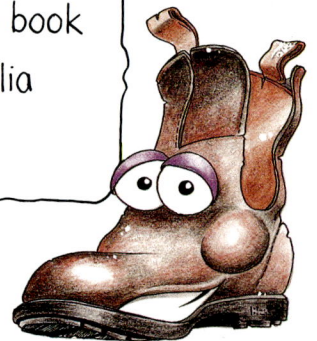

What is wool?

Wool is a natural **fibre**. It grows on sheep and is a bit like hair because when you cut it, it grows back. But unlike hair it clings together and is really good for making into things like clothes and carpets.

Wool is great because it's natural and because it's natural it's **environmentally friendly**. Just by eating grass and drinking water sheep can produce a fibre that no scientists, using chemicals, have been able to copy.

As natural as sun and grass.

The 5 areas of farming

It's often easier to research using a flow chart. Find the area you are interested in....

The Source - Sheep

The Farmer

....read the questions, then turn to the page number to find out some answers!

Sheep

Australia has lots of sheep - about one hundred and forty million (140,000,000). That's more than any other country in the world. Farmers who own the sheep often have over 5,000 on their farm! This, of course, means some farms must be very large and they are called properties or sheep stations.

Farmers have sheep for two reasons: to produce **wool** and **meat**. The sheep that grow really good wool are a breed called **Merinos** and three quarters (that's most) of Australia's sheep are Merinos.

We produce more wool than any other country in the world and most of our wool is sold overseas. Our wool is also the best quality (it must be all that sunshine) and is mainly used to make clothes.

Most of the sheep in Australia are called Merinos. They grow very good wool!

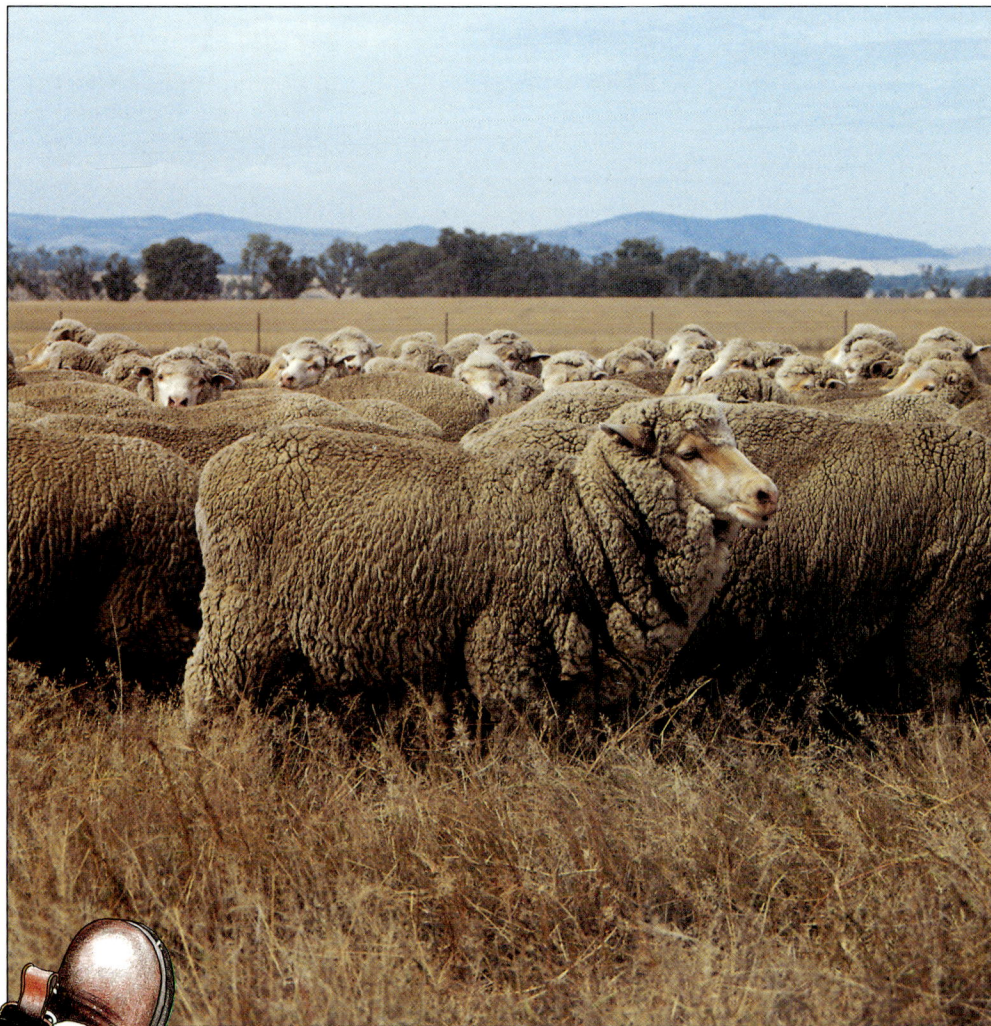

What do you call the first sheep on Mars?

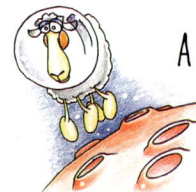

A Mars Baa!

Domestic animals

Sheep are not native to Australia like kangaroos. When the first white people came to live here they brought some sheep with them to use as meat for food. It wasn't long before they discovered what good wool sheep grow here, especially Merinos.

A paddock is an area of land that has been fenced in. In England it is called a field. Each group of sheep in a paddock is called a mob.

Sheep are domestic animals. They depend on the farmer to look after them. A good farmer always makes sure the sheep are in well fenced paddocks which have enough grass and water in them.

3 out of 4 sheep in Australia are Merinos.

Ruminants

Sheep are different to us because they, like cows and goats, belong to a group of animals called **ruminants**. They have four stomachs. They can eat lots of grass, only chewing it a little bit, and it will go into the first part of the stomach where it is stored. Later they can regurgitate (bring up) a ball of grass called a **cud**, and chew on it more thoroughly. This is called "chewing the cud". This allows more saliva and more chewing to break down the food. When they swallow their cud it will then be digested in the last of the four stomachs.

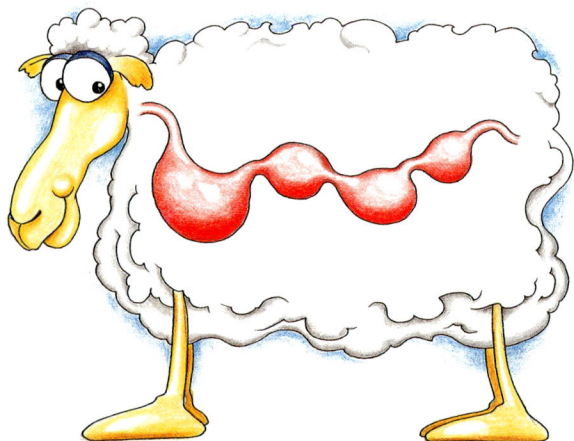

Sheep only eat plant material like grass and seeds.

Sheep spend a lot of their day eating. In fact when they are not sleeping they're usually eating grass or chewing their cud. Sheep spend a lot of time eating because it takes a long time to get enough nutrients or goodness from the grass to help them grow.

These sheep are resting in the shade of a gum tree. While they are doing this they are "chewing their cud" which means they are chewing on some grass they swallowed before.

Teeth

Sheep won't bite you because they are scared of people so they run away if possible. Besides, they only have front teeth on their bottom gum. Having no teeth on their top gum lets the sheep get close to the ground to graze. They have 32 teeth altogether with their molars (back teeth) on top and bottom.

It's easy to tell how old a sheep is by looking at its front teeth (incisors). You count the second or permanent teeth - not the baby teeth.

AGE OF SHEEP

two teeth = one year old

four teeth = two years old

six teeth = three years old

eight teeth = four years old

When sheep get to be about five or six years old their teeth start to break and they can't eat properly. These sheep are called "broken mouthed" and are sold.

Sheep can live until they are about ten years old but most farmers won't keep them this long.

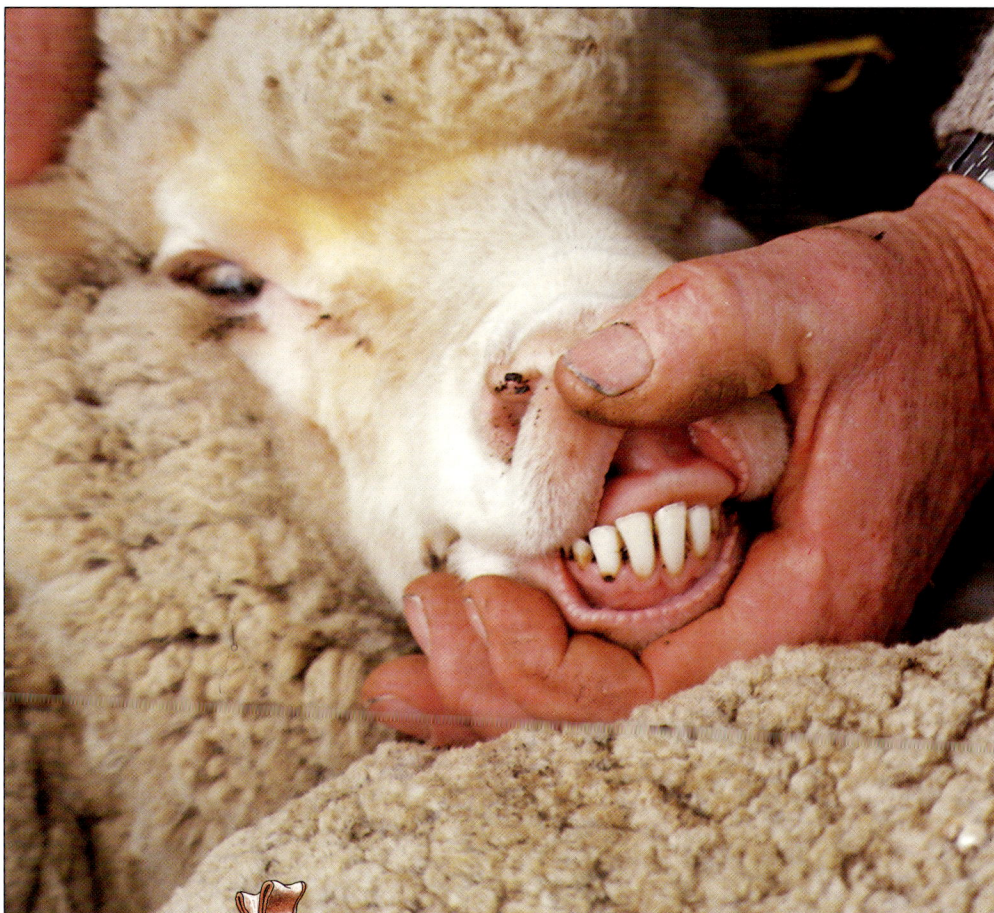

No matter how close I get to these sheep they won't bite me. They would rather eat grass than an old leather boot!

Ewes

A female sheep is called a ewe. (You say that like "you".) Although the farmer gets lots of wool from the ewes their main purpose is to have a lamb each year. They sometimes have twins. When a lamb is playing, the ewe can call it and the lamb knows which voice is its mother's and will come running back.

A lamb is wet when it is born and the ewe knows to lick her baby dry. This not only stops the lamb getting sick if it's a cold, windy day but it also forms a bond between them.

Lambs

Baby sheep are quite strong when they are born. They can walk straight away and soon go off and play with the other lambs in the warm sunshine.

Like you when you were a baby, lambs suck milk and it's really important that they get their first drink soon after they are born because the ewe's milk contains something special called **colostrum** which stops the lamb getting diseases.

Sometimes, but luckily not very often, the ewe might die. If the lamb cannot be matched with another ewe the farmer's children get to **"poddy"** it. They must feed it milk from a bottle two or three times a day. The lambs soon grow to be strong and butt hard against the bottle so it's quite a game not to be pushed over! It's fun to have a poddy lamb.

How do you call out to a girl sheep?

HEY! EWE! HA HA HA HA HA

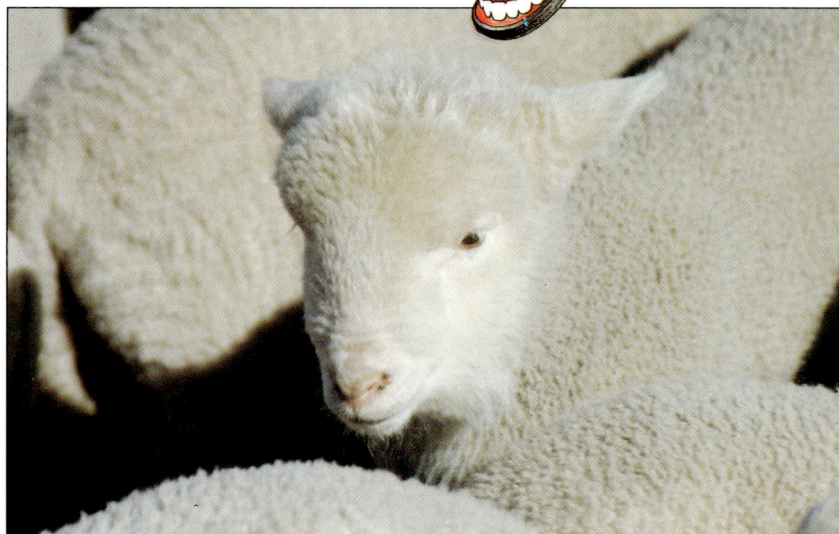

Wethers

Most farmers run big mobs of wethers. These are male sheep that have been **castrated**. This means when they are lambs their testicles (balls) are removed so that instead of growing up to be big, strong rams they will put their energy into growing lots of wool. Wethers are much easier for the farmer to look after than rams.

I wonder whether the wether will like the wet weather?

Rams

Rams are male sheep that are used to produce lambs. As each ram can be mated with about 60 ewes the farmer only needs a small number of them.

This is just as well because rams can be very stubborn! Rams like to show they are tough and sometimes fight each other. They put their heads down and charge - their heads hit with a very loud bang!

They also try to show the sheep dogs "who's the boss" by putting their heads down and stamping their feet when the dogs try to move them.

These rams have been bought from a sheep stud where rams and ewes are specially bred for the wool they grow and for their body size and shape.

The Farmer

What do children do on a farm?

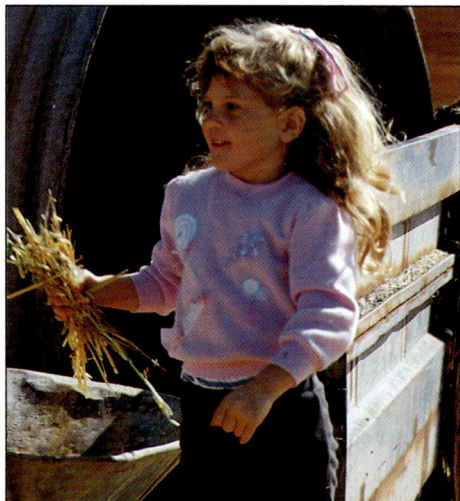

One of the good things about living on a farm would be having your own horse or a small motorbike and a big space in which to ride it. It's fun to be able to help with the work on the farm too. Most kids on farms see more of their parents, especially their dad, than many city children do. This is because it's easy to be with them when they're working. It's a bit harder if your mum or dad works in a factory or an office.

When you live on a farm it's like having a very big playground, with no worries about stranger danger. There's always lots of outdoor things to do like making cubbies, forts and bridges. However, there are also lots of dangers on a farm and children must be very careful to stay well away from any dams, big machinery and silos.

Sometimes it's really busy and there's lots to do, such as at shearing time. It's usually very exciting with so many extra people around. It's great fun to lie in the big bins full of soft fleeces or to climb on the enormous bales of wool.

Farm kids often have chores to do at home, as well as feeding their pets - things like feeding the chooks or picking some vegetables from the plants in the vegetable garden. And of course sometimes there are poddy (motherless) lambs to look after.

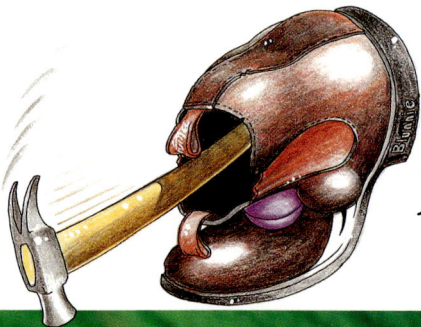

Farm kids see lots of their parents because they can help with the work.

Children are children everywhere so when you live on a farm a lot of the things are the same as if you live in the city. Children still have to go to school. Sometimes the nearest town is far away so it's a long bus ride each day. For other children there might be a school close by but it may be very small with only one teacher and about 18 children. This means you could be in one room with children from every year level.

On some of the really big sheep stations in the outback it's too far to go to a school so the children have Distance Education. They do their school work from home. The children usually have a room in the house set up as the school room and here they do written work which has been sent to them by their teacher. The teachers work in a building in a big city so can't see their students.

This type of schooling is also called School of the Air because each

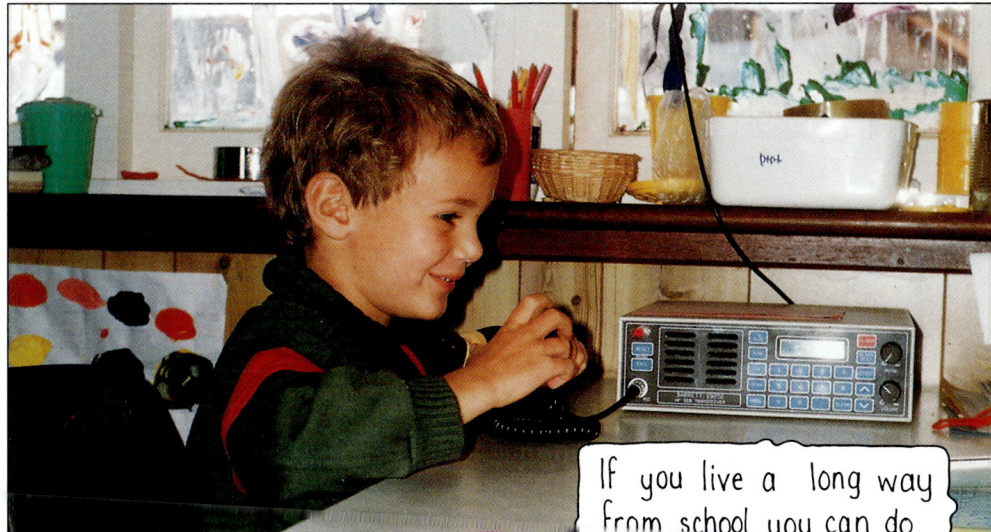

family has a two-way radio and the children can talk to their teacher over the radio. Even though the students in each class can't see each other, they do get to be friends because there is a "galah session" each day where the children can chat amongst themselves over the radio. At different times of the year they get together on someone's sheep station or at the school in the city and do activities like drama, science and sport.

If you live a long way from school you can do your work by radio!

Besides school lots of other things are just the same for country and city kids. Everyone likes to play and inside activities such as Lego, TV and reading are no different. Lots of the outside games are the same too, except most farm children have a bit more space.

Living so far from everyone can be annoying at times and even the children who live on farms near towns don't see their friends much. You can't just go over to someone's house and play, nor can you walk down to the corner shop for an icecream! Also the roads on farms are a bit rough for the things city children do, like skateboarding or roller blading.

Luckily, there are lots of little things about living on a farm that make it fun. It's great to go for a ride in the back of the ute, holding on tight, with the wind streaming through your hair and the dogs panting beside you. Bush barbeques beside the creek, with no other houses or people to be seen are special and so is the sight of a baby lamb, just born, taking its first staggering steps.

Why did the girl throw a glass of milk over the poddy lamb?

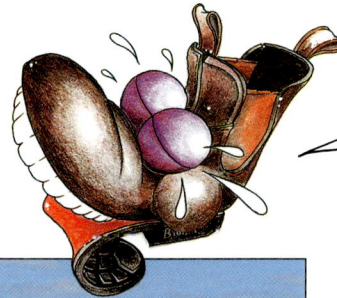

She wanted a Milky Baa! HA HA HA HA HA HA HA

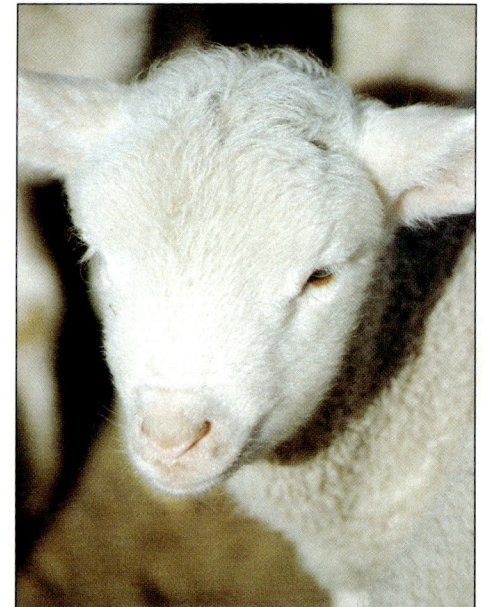

Looking after the sheep

There's always lots of work to be done. You can't just sit back and watch the sheep growing wool!

Sheep need medicine and they also have to have some operations. Sometimes some of the things done to the sheep seem a bit cruel but if they weren't done the sheep could get much sicker later on. This is a bit like giving a baby an injection. It's awful to hear the baby cry so much but we all know it would be much worse if there was no injection and later on the baby got a disease.

A good farmer treats the sheep kindly, working them calmly and quietly so they don't get distressed.

Most sheep farms are run by a family and there are always lots of jobs the children can do. Any child who is willing to help open the gates is always welcome on a trip around the farm. It's always very important to make sure a gate is left exactly as you find it. If it's closed - you must close it after you've gone into the paddock. You can imagine what would happen if you left it open.

Sheep jump when they go through a gate. Farmers sometimes need to count the sheep in a mob. They usually count them by twos.

The farmer must care for all the sheep to make sure they remain healthy and will be able to grow good wool.

Sheep dogs

We mustn't forget the sheep dogs when we talk about looking after the sheep because they're a special part of nearly every farm.

Farmers use Kelpies or Border Collies. These dogs are bred to work with sheep and often the farmer only has to whistle and they know exactly what to do.

Out in the paddocks they help push the sheep into one large mob and direct them towards the gate. They can also get one sheep from the mob by itself so the farmer can look at it.

In the sheep yards the dogs help to move the sheep forward. They can be taught to run along the sheeps' backs, from the front of the mob to the back.

Sheep dogs can actually balance and run on the sheeps' backs!

Blunnie's Farm

KEY

⊥	–	FENCE LINES
ᴗ	–	DAMS
⊥⌐	–	GATES
▢	–	SHEEP YARDS
▪	–	BUILDINGS
▰	–	WINDBREAKS
🌳	–	TREES
⋋	–	CREEKS
╱	–	ROAD

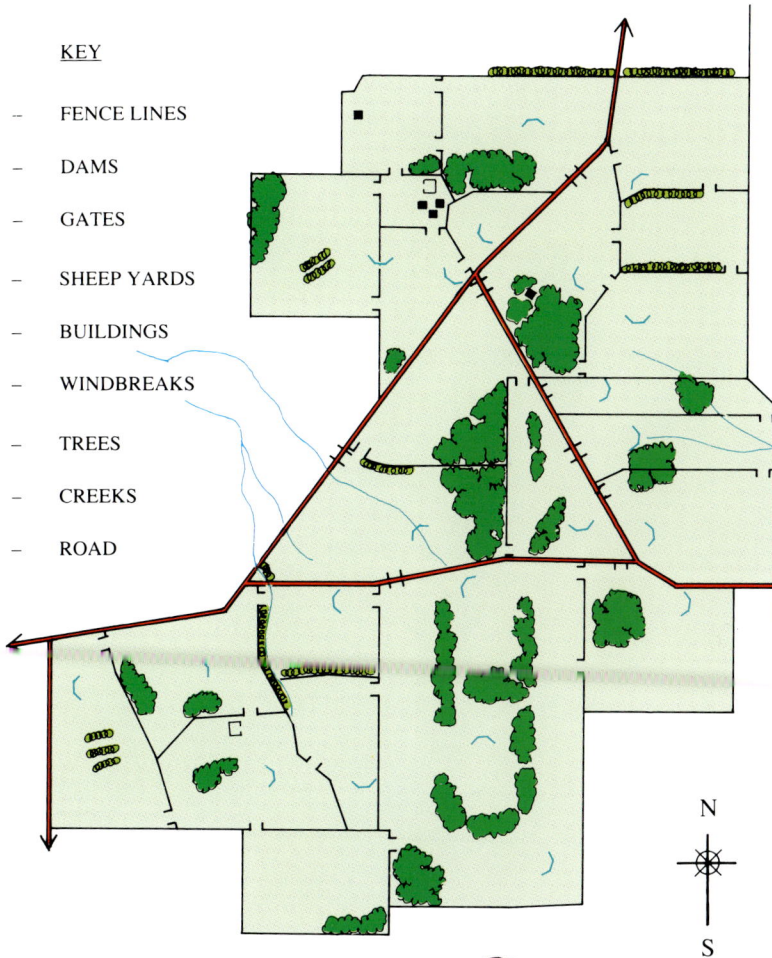

N / S

In the paddocks

The total number of sheep on a farm is called the flock. The farmer sorts the flock of sheep into mobs according to their age and sex. The mobs are put into separate paddocks as this makes it much easier to look after them.

What do you call a ram with b.o. ?

Rambo!

This is a plan of a farm a bit like looking down onto your Lego set up on the floor. You have to imagine you're sitting up on a cloud and looking down you can see the whole farm!

By reading the key you can find out where the gates are and where the water is in each paddock.

What was the sheep doing on the road to the farm?

A ewe turn!
YUK! YUK! YUK!

Mustering

Sheep often have to be moved from their paddocks. This might be because they have eaten most of the grass and they need to go to a new paddock where there have been no sheep.

Another reason to move sheep might be because they need medicine. Of course they won't stand still in the paddock so they have to be brought into some sheep yards.

People don't always ride horses to muster the sheep. Lots of people use motorbikes, utes or small trucks. Nearly everyone has sheep dogs to help.

It's important to have more than one person mustering in a very big paddock. This makes it easier to check all the areas where some sheep might be hiding, such as in a creek or behind a clump of trees. It also stops the sheep that have already been found running back again!

By going into a paddock with their parents, children soon learn how careful you must be to get a "clean muster" - that is not to leave any sheep behind.

The largest muster on record was in Queensland in 1886. 27 men on horses (they didn't let women help in the olden days) moved 43,000 sheep 64km from one sheep station to another. Taking sheep out on the roads is called droving.

Mustering means to go out into the paddock and round up the sheep.

Drafting

This is where the sheep are separated into smaller groups in the sheep yards. You can't just tell sheep which group to go into (so it would be handy for school children too!).

When the sheep are brought into the yards they are put in one big yard at the back.

Next the sheep are moved into the smaller yards with the help of dogs. The whole mob won't fit.

The sheep run along the long narrow drafting race and the farmer moves a gate at the end which directs the sheep into different yards.

See how the ewes are being drafted into the pen on the left and their lambs are all going into the other pen. This makes it easier to work with the lambs.

These are special sheep yards which can be moved out to the paddock - they are portable. It means the sheep don't have to walk too far.

The trick is to get the first sheep running - then the rest will follow because sheep like to play follow the leader.

Lamb operations

Because blowfly strike is such a bad problem in Australia, it's important to make sure the sheep don't have a wet, dirty bottom. That's a place flies love to lay their eggs. With lots of wool around their bottom all the dags (poo) cling on and it gets quite yucky. To stop this happening the lambs have their **tails taken off** and they also have the wrinkly skin around their bottom cut off. This is called **mulesing** and when it heals the skin will be smooth and no wool will grow on it. It helps to keep the sheep clean.

The male lambs are **castrated** although some farmers may keep a few of the best looking ones to become rams.

All the lambs are **earmarked**. They have a hole made in their ear and this shows the farmer's own mark. A coloured tag is used to show the sex and age of the sheep. Ear tags make it easier for the farmer to recognise the group the sheep belongs to (like school uniforms). Earmarking is like having your ears pierced but the

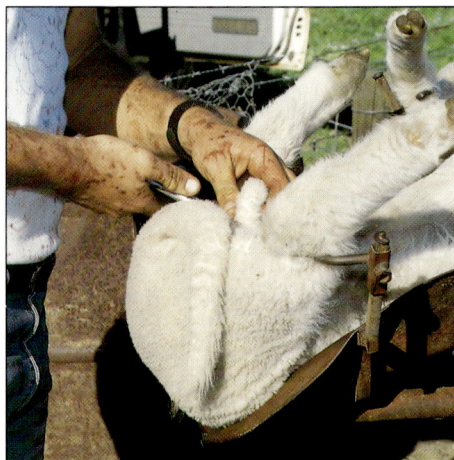

sheep never get to wear gold earrings!

The lambs have to be **vaccinated** against disease now that they are six weeks old, as the colostrum they got from their mother's milk doesn't protect them any longer. Colostrum contains special substances called antibodies. Antibodies fight diseases and infections.

When the lambs are about 6 weeks old they have some operations to help them stay healthy as they get older — the operations don't hurt too much.

When the operations are over the lambs and ewes find each other again by bleating (calling out), and they are put back into their paddock together.

Vaccinating

Just like you have to have needles to prevent you getting some diseases like measles, so do sheep. The farmer brings the sheep into the sheep yards and moves them into a long narrow yard called a **race**. They can't move much and are easy to handle safely. The sheep are then injected with a measured amount of medicine (vaccine) using a needle. It goes under the skin and sheep don't seem to feel it.

A vet isn't needed to give these injections - it's easy enough for the farmer to do. Anyway just imagine taking a whole mob of sheep into the vet clinic!

Sheep are given needles to stop them getting diseases — but I didn't think boots needed vaccinating!

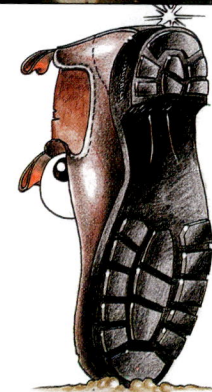

Parasites

Parasites are small living creatures that live on or in the sheep and can make them very sick or even kill them. Worms, maggots and lice are all parasites. It is important that the farmer controls the parasites in the sheep flock, not only for the sheep's sake, but also because a sick sheep is not going to produce as much wool as a healthy sheep.

Wherever possible, the farmer tries to prevent the sheep getting the parasites in the first place, rather than having to use chemicals to cure them.

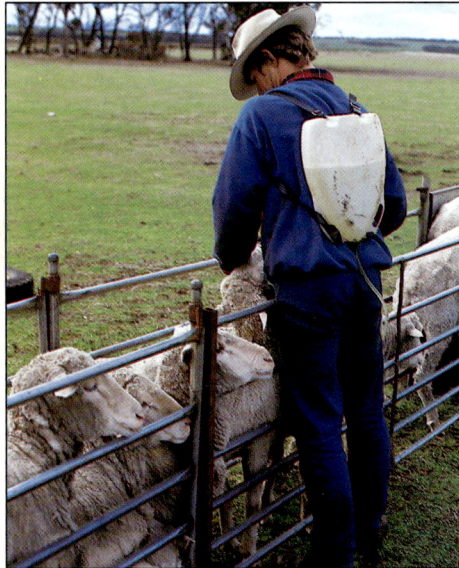

They can do this by keeping the soil healthy and by being careful about where they put the sheep. Farm chemicals are expensive so farmers only use them when they are really needed.

Drenching

Sheep need to take medicine to control worms just like you have to sometimes.

The farmer has the medicine, called **drench**, in a backpack like you can see in the picture below.

With the backpack on, a measured amount of drench is then squirted down the sheep's throat with the thing that looks like a water pistol.

Because the race is narrow the farmer can easily reach all the sheep to drench them.

The sheep are let out the end when they have been drenched. The gate is closed and the race is refilled with more sheep from the mob.

Sheep won't open wide to take their medicine.

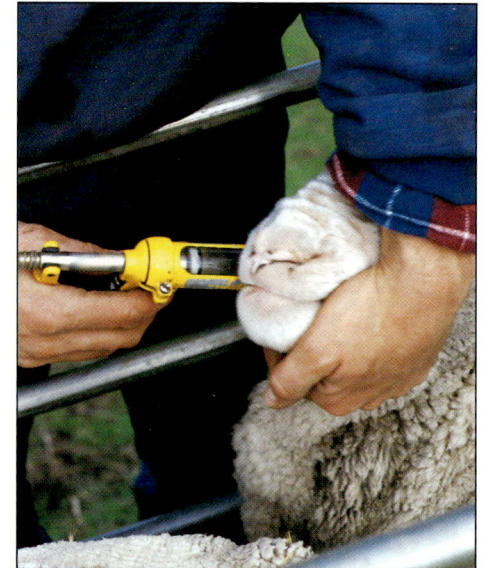

Once or twice a year sheep must be given medicine (drenched) to kill worms which grow inside them. These worms can make sheep very sick and can even kill them.

Dipping or backlining

Other parasites that can be a problem are **lice**. They are small insects that live in the sheep's wool near the skin. They make the sheep very itchy and the sheep then rub themselves against fences and trees. This ruins their wool.

Lice spend their whole lives on the sheep so the farmer is able to remove them completely from the flock by using a chemical treatment on the sheep. Sometimes we get lice in our hair and have to use a chemical to kill them.

The best time to treat the sheep is after shearing because their wool is very short and the insects can't hide. The farmer can either pour a chemical in a line along the sheep's back **(backlining)** or get the sheep to walk through a shower or swim through a special bath filled with the chemical **(dipping)**.

Some insects, like lice, can make sheep very itchy. The sheep can ruin their wool trying to scratch, so the lice must be killed.

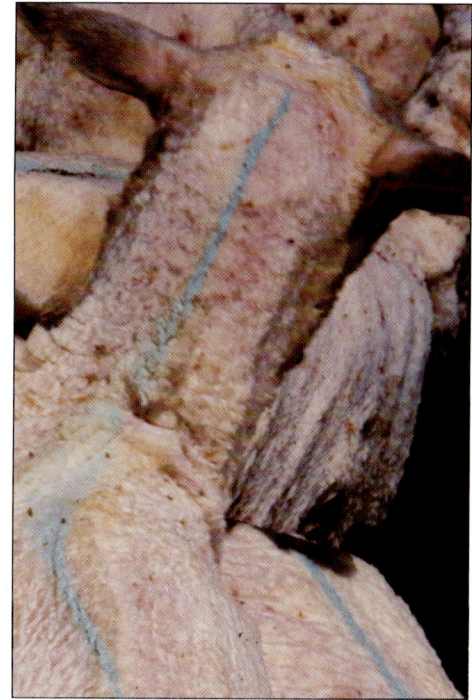

Blowfly control

In Australia, the blowfly is one of the biggest sheep health problems. In the spring time, blowflies get into parts of the sheep's wool that are moist because of urine (wee) and lay their eggs. Maggots hatch out of the eggs.

You may have seen maggots before - they are small, white grubs laid by flies which wriggle madly. These maggots bite into the sheep's skin using hooks in their mouths and, as you can imagine, make nasty wounds. Not only can this ruin the sheep's fleece but the wound can get infected and the sheep can die. This is all quite horrible so it's important to try to stop the sheep getting fly blown.

Mulesing and taking the tails off the lambs helps to stop blowflies hurting sheep because it means there is less wool around the sheep's bottom that can get dirty or wet. **Crutching** the sheep also helps to prevent fly strike. Crutching means that the wool around the bottom is shorn.

Sometimes sheep get struck by blowflies on the main part of their bodies. If it has been raining for days, the sheep's skin can get infected. This is called **fleece rot**. It smells very nasty and blowflies love it! Warm, wet weather allows lots of flies to hatch out.

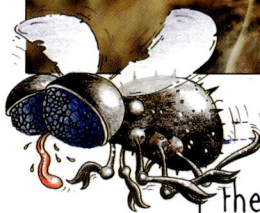

When blowfly maggots bite into the sheep's skin it gets infected. Farmers say the sheep is fly blown or fly struck

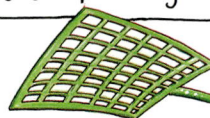

A female fly lives for 7 weeks. In that time she can produce 7,000 maggots!

If some sheep do get struck then they must be treated quickly.

The farmer uses a liquid chemical that can be poured onto the wound to kill the maggots. If many sheep are struck then the whole mob will have to be treated.

Instead of trying to pour the liquid all over each sheep it's much easier to get them to walk through something like a shower but instead of plain water it's a special chemical mixed with water. The sheep's wool gets soaked and the liquid will kill any maggots that hatch in the wool for up to 12 weeks. The liquid will not harm the sheep or the wool but it must be used carefully.

It is impossible to get rid of the problem of blowfly strike by killing all the flies - Australia has too many of them! So the farmers must do things to prevent the sheep being struck and must treat the sheep quickly if they do get fly struck.

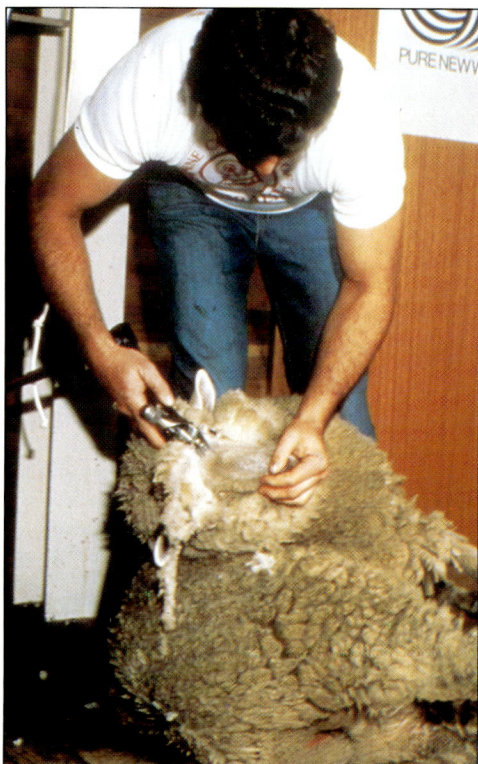

Crutching and wigging

Sometimes during the year, a little bit of shearing, of certain parts of the body, must be done to keep the sheep healthy.

Cutting stained wool away from around the sheep's bottom and back legs is called **crutching**. This area can get covered in **dags**. It must be kept clean to help prevent fly strike. Ewes are usually crutched just before they have their lambs.

Cutting the wool away from around the sheep's eyes is called **wigging**. This is like having your fringe cut. In summer time grass seeds can get in this wool and can work their way into the sheep's eyes where they often get stuck. They can make the sheep go blind. Wigging the sheep helps with both the problem of grass seeds and fly strike.

Sometimes during the year the sheep have some wool shorn from around their faces and their bottoms. Guess which one is called wigging.

Controlling footrot

Footrot is a major sheep disease in Australia. The sheep get an infection in their feet and become lame. They limp when walking.

Footrot can spread very quickly. The infection can live for about a week in the ground. If one mob of sheep on the farm gets footrot it is important that they are treated and kept away from other sheep so the infection won't spread.

The farmer can pare (cut) the sheep's toenails and get the sheep to walk through and stand in a "footbath" full of a chemical that helps kill the infection. However, if the footrot is really bad then it can't be cured and the sheep must be sold to the abattoirs where they are killed.

When sheep get footrot their feet get sore and they can't walk very well.

Why did the ram jump off the cliff?

Because he heard someone singing "There'll never be another you!"

Shearing

Sheep are shorn once a year. Shearing is probably the most exciting time of the year. Everyone is busy and an important job is being done. Some farmers can shear their own sheep but most get in a team of specially trained **shearers**.

On some farms, particularly in the outback, it's too far for the shearers to go home each night so they stay near the shearing shed in the shearers' quarters - a set of small rooms with a big kitchen and a dining room called the mess. These teams have a cook with them and it's always fun to go into the kitchen especially near smoko when there are huge cakes being made. The smell is wonderful!

Shearers still call morning and afternoon tea smoko even though most of them probably don't smoke any more.

Before shearing the farmer must bring the mobs of sheep in from the paddocks. They are usually put in the sheep yards overnight to empty out (do lots of poo). If it

looks like it's going to rain the sheep have to be put in small yards inside the shearing shed because the shearers won't shear wet sheep.

Early in the morning the farmer must move the sheep into small pens behind each shearer ready for the day's work. During the day the pens must be refilled. Children often help to "pen up" and they

sometimes help out the front, sweeping up little pieces of wool.

A Merino wether got lost in the bush in NSW for 5 years and when it was found its wool was 46cm long! That's as long as this book!

The Shearer

Each shearer goes into a pen, drags out a sheep, sits it up, holding it firmly and then begins to shear using mechanical cutters, a bit like the hairdresser can use to shave the back of your neck. The first bits to come off are the short pieces around the head and the belly. These are usually a bit stained and are kept separate from the main **fleece**. Because wool fibres cling to each other when the sheep is shorn the rest of the fleece comes off in one piece.

Shearers can hurt their backs from bending over all day so some shearers use a supportive sling that hangs from the ceiling.

After the sheep is shorn the shearer pushes it down a chute like a slippery dip and it goes into a yard with other sheep shorn by that shearer. The sheep have to be counted because shearers get paid for the number of sheep they shear during the day. The fastest shearer (the ringer or gun shearer) will make the most money.

Sheds used to have up to 20 shearers working at once but now there are usually only four or five.

Shearing used to be done by hand with blades like big scissors. A man called Jackie Howe holds the record for being the fastest shearer. He was the ringer at Alice Downs station in Queensland in 1892. Once he managed to shear 321 sheep in a day (8 hours and 40 minutes).

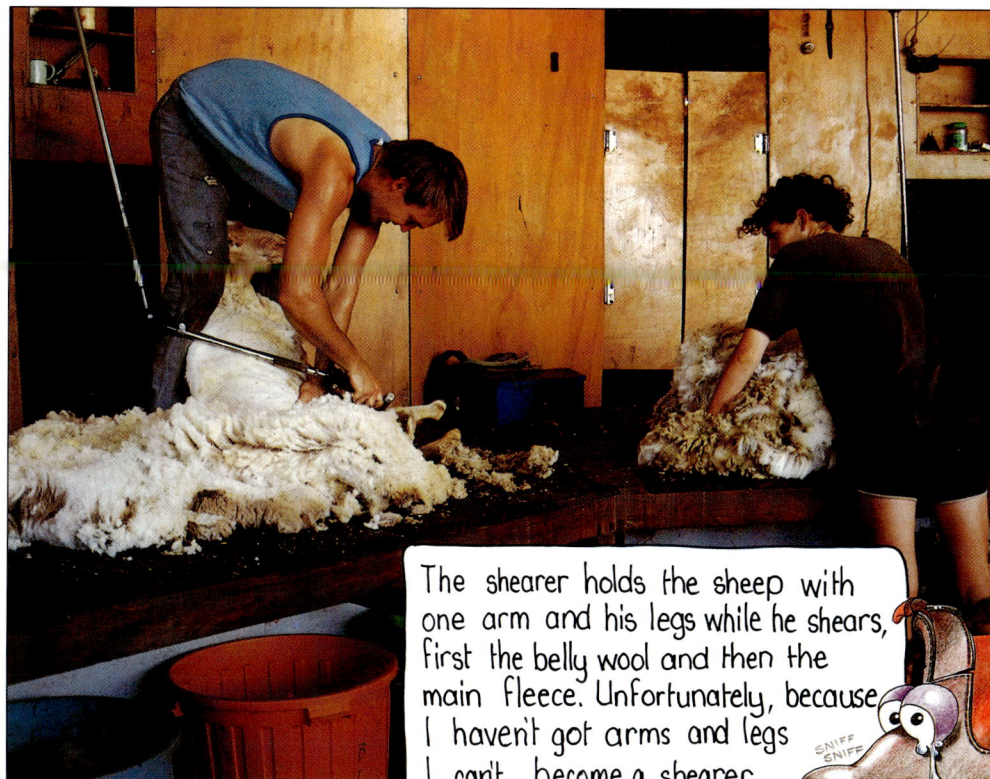

The shearer holds the sheep with one arm and his legs while he shears, first the belly wool and then the main fleece. Unfortunately, because I haven't got arms and legs I can't become a shearer.

The Rouseabout

The **rouseabout**, or shedhand, picks up the fleece from the **board** and throws it over a table, like throwing a sheet over a bed. He or she helps the classer to **skirt** it. The rouseabout helps in other ways such as sweeping the floor to keep it free from small pieces of wool and penning up more sheep for the shearers.

The classer has a look at the fleece and decides what sort of quality it is. He then puts it in a "class" or "group."

The Classer

The fleece is skirted by the **classer**. This means the outside pieces are removed because they are not of as good a quality as the rest and they are put with the other shorter wool.

The classer is a person who groups the wool according to how it feels and what it looks like. He or she looks at both the **colour** and the **crimp**. Sometimes the wool breaks easily. This is called tender wool and it is not worth as much money as other wool.

The classer puts the wool into special bins so fleeces of the same type go together. The classer is usually the boss of the shearing team.

In the olden days men used to wear powdered wigs made of wool. So to "pull the wool over someone's eyes" meant to trick them because you'd pull down their wig so they couldn't see what was happening.

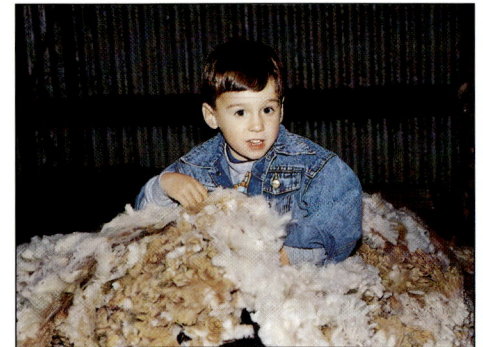

It's fantastic fun to jump into these bins full of lovely soft wool.

The Presser

The **presser** is a person who collects a group of the same sort of fleeces and puts them into a mechanical press to make a **bale** of wool. The press squashes the wool down really tightly and then seals the bale so it can't all pop out again! The presser must be careful nothing else accidentally gets in the bale with the lovely, white fleeces. A bale of wool is higher than you and fits about 40 fleeces in it. It's really heavy (about 200kg) and is hard to move.

Each bale is marked with the name of the property and the type of fleece it contains. The bales are stacked ready to be taken to a wool centre where they will be sold. The wool, straight off the sheep's back,

is called **greasy wool** because it still has the wool grease or lanolin in it and is very soft.

The first shearing machine in the world was developed in Australia in 1885. At the time, it was no faster than blade shearing but it got much closer to the skin so got more wool from the sheep.

The first complete shearing by machine anywhere in the world was at Dunlop Station, Louth NSW in 1888.

> The presser uses a machine to squash the wool into bales

Other work to be done on the farm

Sheep farmers have to do lots of other work as well as the work they do with the sheep.

In the paddocks

Gates and fences must be kept in good order otherwise the mobs of sheep will get boxed (mixed up).

Each paddock must have water in it for the sheep to drink. Sometimes there is a creek but in Australia most of our creeks only have water in them after a lot of rain. To put water in each paddock the farmer can dig a dam which will hold rainwater.

They can put in a bore. On many outback sheep stations there isn't enough rainwater to fill a dam so people put large pipe into the underground water. It doesn't taste very good but the animals don't mind.

Or they can put in a trough. A pipe under the ground carries water to the trough from water in another paddock, such as in a dam or from the bore.

To enable the farmer to have even more sheep, in areas where there is lots of rain, farmers have improved the **pastures** by planting lucerne and clover. These aren't really grasses but something called legumes. Farmers add fertiliser to them and they grow even more!

In the outback, there's not much rain so there's not much grass. Sheep stations are very large.

Sometimes farmers need to give the sheep extra food. They are usually fed hay or grain such as oats which is expensive to buy. This happens in droughts when there hasn't been enough rain for the grass to grow, or on some farms in summer when there isn't much grass.

Some farmers make large bales of hay in the spring when the grass is long and the sheep can't eat it all. They use these to feed the sheep over the dry summer months or in a drought. The bales are very big, about two times as tall as you. The farmer needs a tractor with a big fork on the front to move the bales to the paddock where the sheep can eat them.

The farm on the left has lots of grass and needs only a small area to feed one sheep. If there's less grass, the sheep need a bigger area.

There must be enough food for the sheep to eat. The number of sheep that can be put on a farm depends on the pasture (grass) that grows there.

At the sheds

On every farm there are a group of sheds in which to keep the machinery and a workshop with tools for fixing things. Farmers look after their machinery (trucks, tractors, motor bikes) themselves. They don't have a mechanic close by to do it.

Farmers are running a business. They must spend time working at a desk.

At the house

Like all business people, farmers must spend some time at a desk doing paperwork. There are plans to be made about how to run the farm, records to be kept about the sheep and of course there are always bills to pay. Lots of farmers use a computer and fax machine to help them.

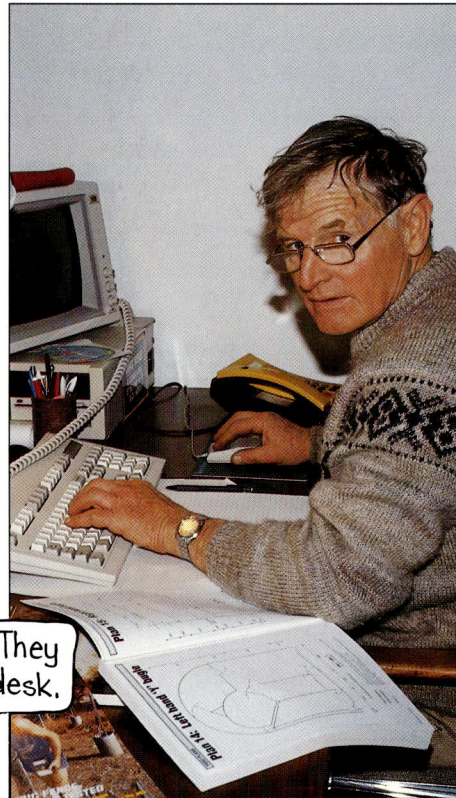

Off the farm

Someone from the family must go into town to buy things, like drench or fencing equipment that are needed on the farm. Country towns have developed to supply the local farmers and the shop keepers only make money if the farmers are making money.

Farmers also go to sheep sales and field days. A field day is when a group of farmers go into a paddock to look at new machinery or new methods of doing things. Because we don't have fields here - we're not in England after all - they should really be called paddock days!

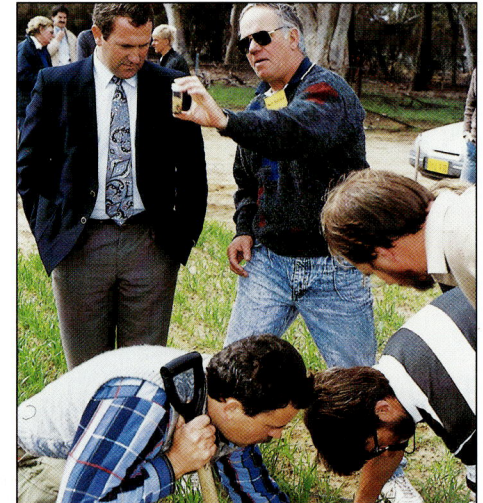

Buying and selling sheep

At different times during the year the farmer will have to either buy or sell sheep. If the season is good, more sheep can be put on the property but if it's bad there isn't enough grass and often some will be sold. Old sheep and ewes that do not have lambs are drafted out and sold.

Sheep are usually sold at big saleyards in a nearby town. An auction is held and the person who bids the most (offers the most money) buys the sheep.

Sheep are also sold through CALM - Computer Aided Livestock Marketing. Instead of

What do you call a cheap sheep? A baa-gain!

taking the sheep to the saleyards the sellers list their sheep and things about them such as how much they weigh, on a computer. The buyers all have computers too and can read this. When the auction is held they type in their bid for the mob of sheep they want to buy.

The most expensive sheep ever bought: Richard Nitschke paid $450,000 to own 3/4 of a ram called Collinsville Lustre 53. The sheep was worth $600,000.

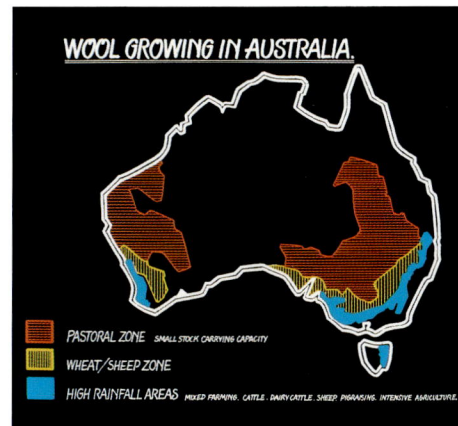

WOOL GROWING IN AUSTRALIA.

PASTORAL ZONE SMALL STOCK CARRYING CAPACITY

WHEAT/SHEEP ZONE

HIGH RAINFALL AREAS MIXED FARMING. CATTLE. DAIRY CATTLE. SHEEP. PIG RAISING. INTENSIVE AGRICULTURE.

Abattoirs

Most sheep end up at an abattoir. This is a place where sheep are killed for meat for us to eat and for tins of pet food. Some people also grow prime lambs specially for meat. These are another breed and they are bigger and fatter than Merinos and they don't produce wool as good as that produced by a Merino.

We buy the meat from butchers and supermarkets. Usually it's labelled **lamb** (like lamb chops or lamb roast) but if the sheep was an older one, the meat is called **mutton**.

Meat from an adult sheep is called mutton!

Farm safety

It's important to make farming as safe as possible. Every year people hurt themselves and in most cases it can be avoided.

The major problems on a sheep farm are:

Zoonoses - these are diseases that people can catch from animals.

If you get a cut after handling diseased sheep it should be cleaned and disinfected .

Hydatids is a disease caused by tapeworm which dogs can get from eating sheep offal (liver, kidney etc). It doesn't affect dogs but dogs can transfer hydatids to people, which can make them very sick.

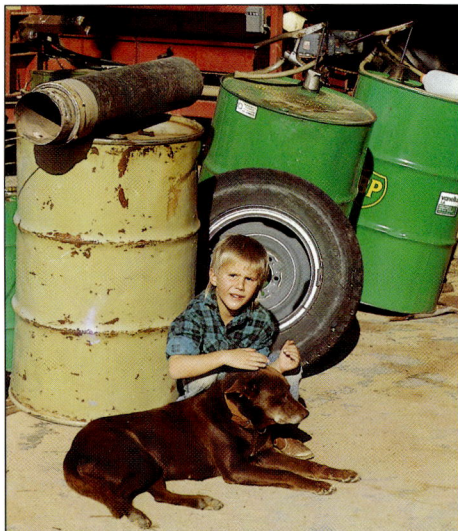

Don't let dogs eat raw offal and give them tapeworm tablets. Always wash your hands before you eat!

Being hit by sheep - rams can charge and bang into knees, small horns can jab into hands.

Treat all sheep with respect, learn how they will react in the sheep yards and be ready for their movements.

Lifting sheep the wrong way backs can be hurt by lifting sheep and other heavy objects incorrectly.

Knees should be bent and backs straight when lifting. If it's possible, put the sheep through a gate instead of lifting them over a fence.

Skin cancer - farmers spend most of their day outside in the sun so they must wear adequate protection.

It's important to be careful on the farm. Many farmers hurt themselves because they don't pay enough attention to farm safety.

In NSW a man called Graham Robertson was paring his sheep's feet and he accidentally cut off the end of his thumb with the very sharp cutters. He bent down to pick it up so he could take it to the hospital and have it sewn back on. Just as he was about to get this part of his thumb, his dog ran over and ate it! (That's a yucky story but it's true!)

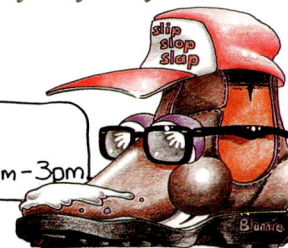

Always wear a hat and 15+ sunscreen. During summer it's best not to work in the sun between 10am-3pm

slip slop slap

Blunnie

WOOL

What happens to wool after it leaves the farm?

Selling the wool

The total number of bales of wool that a farmer has each year is called the **wool clip**. After shearing, the clip from most farms is taken by truck or train to a large wool centre. There are thousands of bales of wool there and samples are taken from each one.

One sample is displayed so the people who buy the wool for the woollen mills can look at it and feel it. They are called wool buyers.

Another sample is sent to a wool testing laboratory so the wool buyer will know the micron measurement of the wool and how clean it is. Finer wool is used for suits and dresses and stronger wool for things like thick jumpers or furnishing fabric, so it's very important that the wool buyer knows as much about the wool as possible.

Tests are also done to see how long and strong the wool is.

The highest price ever paid for any wool was in 1989 for a bale of Tasmanian super fine wool. Some Japanese people paid $3000.50 per kilogram for it. A kilo of wool is about as heavy as a litre of milk but takes up more room. Most people only get about $5 for a kilo of wool.

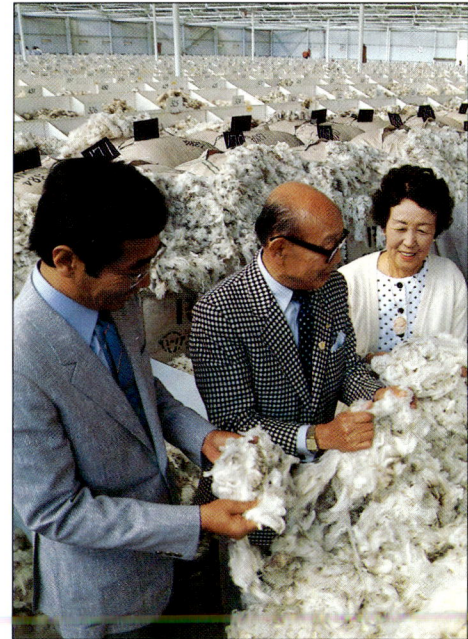

When an auction is held the wool buyers bid against each other for "lots" of wool. The highest bidder gets to buy the wool.

Microns

Wool is grouped according to how thick each fibre is. This is measured in **microns**. There are one thousand microns in one millimetre. If the crimp is very close together the wool is fine and will be less than 20 microns. Medium wool is between 20 and 23 microns. Strong wool will be more than 23 microns.

Who buys Australian wool?

Nearly all our wool (97%) goes overseas. Most Australian wool is between 19 and 23 microns which is very fine compared to wool from other countries. It is very good for clothes. We are the world's largest exporter of wool that is used to make clothes.

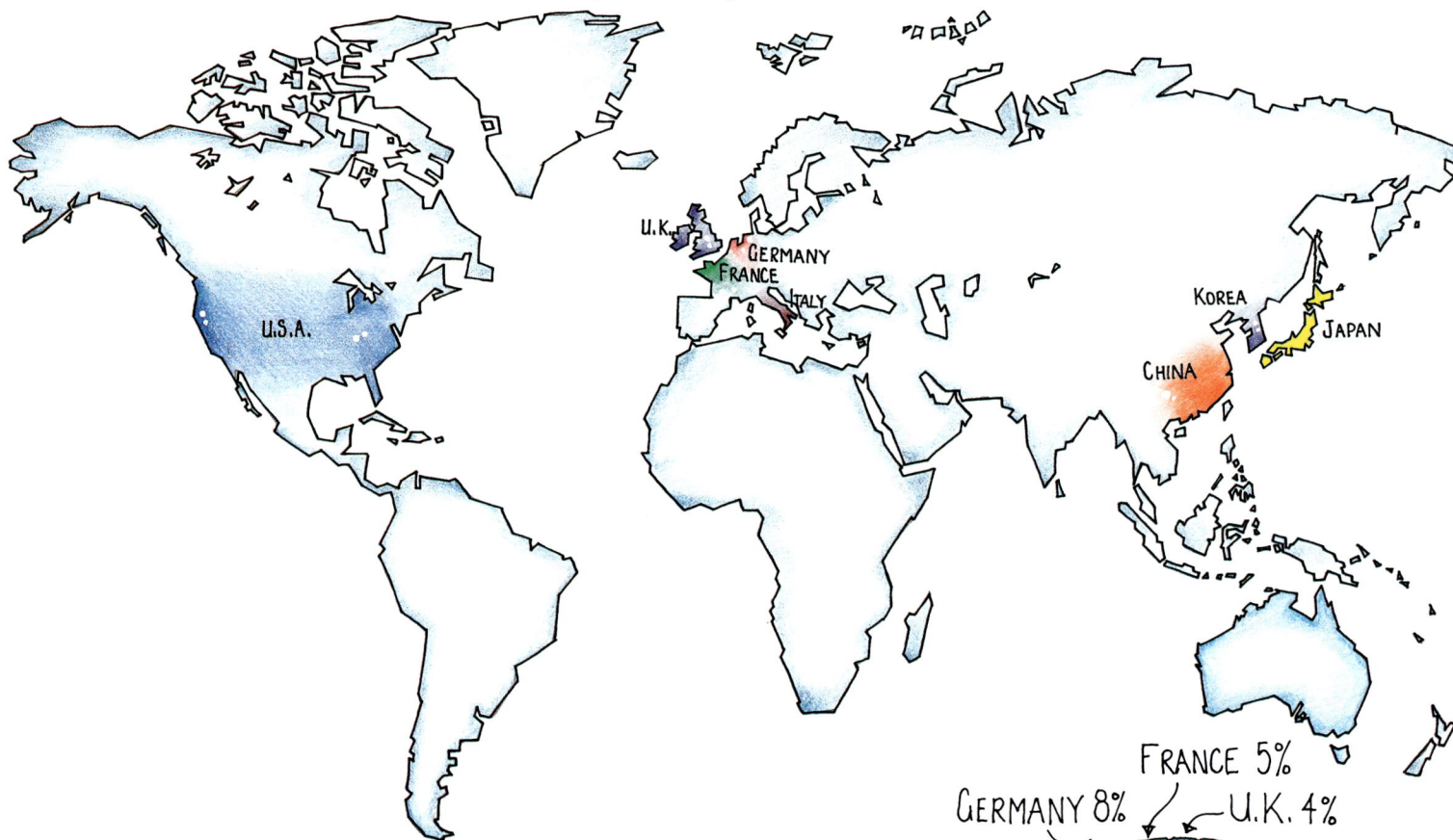

Most of our wool is sold to Asia.

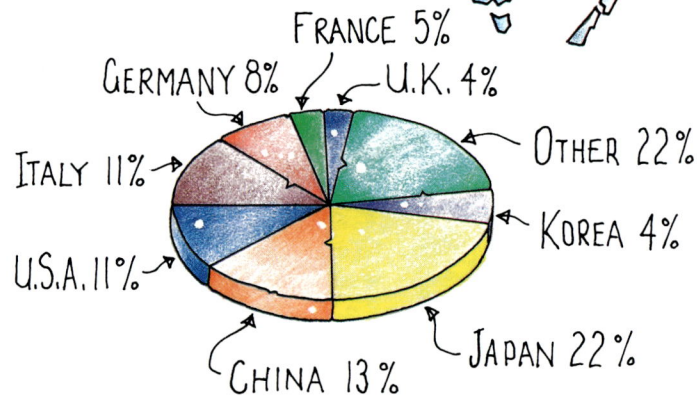

FRANCE 5%
GERMANY 8%
U.K. 4%
ITALY 11%
OTHER 22%
U.S.A. 11%
KOREA 4%
CHINA 13%
JAPAN 22%

Keep the clip clean

It's very important that each farmer's clip contains only fleeces of white wool. Wool that is stained from urine (wee) or wool from a black sheep can ruin the whole bale. If some buyers from Italy want wool to make beautiful clothes they want to know the wool will be fine and white. If there are some black threads in the fabric when it is made up, do you think they will come back to Australia to buy more wool?

Not only is stained wool sometimes put in the bales but here are some other amazing things that have accidentally been included!

- Tea towels
- Spanners
- Bullets
- Clothes
- Money
- Work boots
- Hammers

HELP! HELP! I'm too young to die!

Black sheep may look cute but farmers have to be careful to keep them well away from all their white sheep. One fibre of black wool in a bale can ruin it.

IN & TAMMIN AGRICULTUR

Champion

FLEECE

Processing the wool

Most of our wool goes overseas as greasy wool. Some (20%) is cleaned here and then sent overseas where the processing is finished.

There are two systems used to process wool.

The worsted system uses finer, longer wool and when processed the yarn is used to make suits and dresses. Most (80%) of our wool is used in this system.

The woollen system uses coarser shorter wool and when processed

the yarn is used to make heavier, hairier products like thick jumpers and blankets.

The processing begins with **scouring** (cleaning). The wool is washed and the dirt, sweat, wool grease and any chemicals that might remain in the wool are removed. **Lanolin** is a product taken from wool grease. It is a cream used for our bodies and faces.

Next the wool goes through a number of steps where it is untangled and straightened out. The worsted system is more complex at this stage.

The wool is then spun into long threads by machines. In the olden days this was done by hand on a spinning wheel.

Most wool is dyed a colour after it has been spun into yarn although it can be dyed at any stage.

J. Barker of Western Australia holds the record for the longest thread of hand spun wool. In 1989 she spun some wool that was 553.03 metres long. That thread of wool would reach up and down an Olympic swimming pool eleven times!

Why can't you trust a sheep?

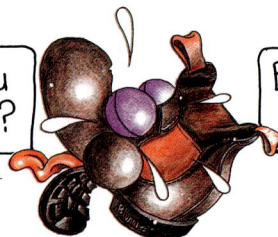

Because they're always spinning yarns!

What is the wool used for?

The wool may be:

- Woven into fabric for suits and dresses.
  The weaving machine is called a loom.

- Knitted on large machines.
  Your jumper may look like this.

- Rolled into balls and sold for hand knitting.

Did you know these things can also be made from wool?

- Firefighters uniforms
- Tennis ball coverings

Wool has even been used to soak up oil from oil spills. That's environmentally friendly!

- The inside of baseballs and cricket balls
- Felt tip pens
- Doonas
- Chalk board dusters
- Sleeping bags
- Piano key hammers
- Flags
- Insulation in the roofs of houses
- Carpets
- Billiard table coverings
- Blankets
- Lining for stereo cabinets
- Felt hats
- Felt lining for the soles of boots
- Tapestry
- Fabric to cover chairs
- Filters to stop oil and dust

In 1982 in Victoria 65 people decided to see how quickly they could make a three piece suit starting from the wool still on the sheep. It only took them 1 hour, 34 minutes and 33.42 seconds! To catch and shear the sheep took just 2 minutes.

Wool and the economy

> The economy means buying and selling things and the money the country makes. We need to sell things to other countries (export) so we can have money to buy the things we want.

> Agriculture (sheep, cattle, wheat, etc) is very important to our economy. It makes up about one third of all the things we export.

Soon after the first white people came here from England they began to produce wool. It was a good product to sell to England because:
- Merino sheep grew lovely, fine wool.
- It didn't get ruined in the long sea voyage.
- There was a big demand for it to make clothes for people in Europe.

For over 100 years, wool was the product that earned the most money for Australia. People used to say we were "riding on the sheep's back". This really means wool supported the country.

Today wool is still an important product for Australia. We export nearly all the wool we grow. Most of it goes to Asia. Wool makes up one tenth of our exports and earns a lot of money for our country.

Wool has always been a very important product for the Australian economy.

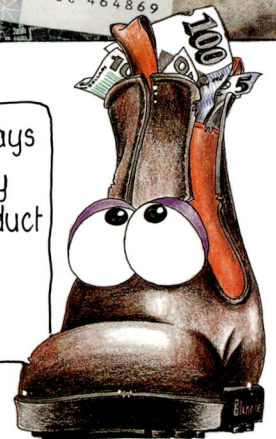

The consumer

Clothes made from wool

Just as wool may be spun and made into clothes so may a variety of natural and synthetic fibres. Cotton and silk are other examples of natural fibres.

A synthetic fibre is one that has been made from chemicals in a factory. This uses a lot of energy and creates a great deal of pollution. Many synthetic fibres, such as nylon and polyester, are man made from oil or coal. Although different synthetics are good for specific things no scientist has yet been able to develop a fibre that is as good as wool in every way.

Wool can also be mixed with other fibres. Wool and lycra is a very popular blend because stretch fabrics are in fashion.

When you buy clothes made in a factory they have a label on them to show you what they are made from. If you see this label called the Woolmark it means your piece of clothing is made from wool that has come from the sheep's back and it is Pure New Wool. This is one of the most widely recognised signs in the world.

The Australian Wool Corporation promotes Australian wool worldwide and also works to maintain the excellent quality of our wool.

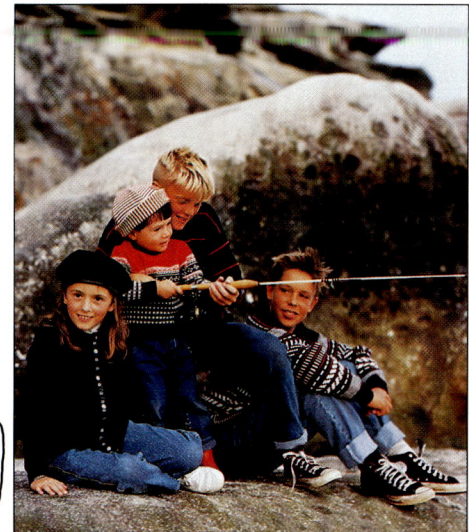

The Woolmark

PURE NEW WOOL

A consumer is a person who buys or uses something. You are a consumer and the Australian Wool Corporation wants you to be happy with the woollen clothes you buy.

The Woolmark label guarantees high quality.

Made in Australia

Check some of your clothes at home to see what the labels say. Can you find some woollen ones? Do they also say Made in Australia? If you buy Australian woollen clothes then you will be helping our country and you'll be wearing the best quality wool in the world.

Anyone who owns at least five pieces of woollen clothing that say Made in Australia on the label deserves a pat on the back and perhaps an icecream!

> It is very important for our country to buy Australian wool. Next time you go shopping for a jumper, socks or jacket make sure to buy one made of wool with a "Made in Australia" label.

AUSTRALIAN MADE

What's so good about wool?

Most people know wool keeps you warm but here are some things about it you may not know.

- **Wool keeps its shape**
  It is springy and will stretch and return to the same shape so it doesn't go baggy like old tracksuits. It doesn't crease either.

  Activity: cut a piece of wool and stretch it then watch it spring back.

- **Wool soaks up moisture**
  If you go outside on a cold, damp day your jumper will soak up the damp air but it won't cling to you so you'll stay dry and warm.

  Activity: blindfolded smell some wet wool and some other wet fabrics.

- **Water rolls off wool**
  Even though it soaks up moisture, if it's really raining the rain will slide off the surface of your woollen jacket so you'll stay dry for quite a while.

Activity: put on two gloves (one wool and one acrylic) and sprinkle one tablespoon of water on each and leave for five minutes. Put each glove on some paper towel and you will see the woollen glove has held the moisture which means it hasn't got on to your skin.

Where do sheep do their shopping?

Woolworths! HA HA HA HA

Why is wool better?

- **Wool doesn't burn easily**
  If you catch on fire and you're wearing wool your clothes won't burst into flames and they won't melt and stick to your skin like many synthetic fibres.
  A woollen blanket will put out a flame very quickly - it can save your life.

- **Wool doesn't get dirty easily**
  Just like rain, dirt doesn't cling to wool. Also, you don't get sparks when you touch it. Wool resists static electricity.

- **Wool keeps you warm in winter and cool in summer**
  It insulates your body so people in hot countries wear it to keep cool and people in cool countries wear it to keep warm.

Wool is great for children because it's so safe near fires!

What have been some of the problems with wool?

• Shrinkage

Some wool shrinks when put in a washing machine.

The CSIRO has developed a process to stop wool shrinking. This is now used worldwide and has meant that some wools can even be washed in a machine.

However, special jumpers must still be carefully washed by hand.

• Moth proofing

Moths can be a problem because they like to eat holes in your woollen clothes when stored in the cupboard. Chemicals can be used to prevent this but the best thing to do is to clean your clothes and put them in a plastic bag - moths can't eat through plastic.

• Prickliness

Lots of children don't like wearing wool next to their skin because it can be prickly. It is the coarse fibres (over 27 microns) in wool that make it prickly. They are quite stiff and stick out, scratching the skin. All wool has some coarse fibres in it. The CSIRO is trying to work out ways to either remove the coarse fibres or cover them up.

Clothes made from fine wools are the best to wear because they don't have many coarse fibres in them.

The Wool Research and Development Corporation is an organisation that sets up programmes with the CSIRO to develop ways to improve the quality of wool products and to make sure sheep farming and the processing of wool doesn't have a negative effect on the environment. Farmers have been putting money into wool research programmes since the 1930's.

Scientists are always trying to make wool a better product for the consumer.

The Environment

Today, more than ever before, people are concerned about the effect we all have on the environment. If we continue to take from the land and not return anything then the land will die. We have come to realise that we must live with the land not from it. This means we must repair any damage that has been done to our environment and we must work to keep it healthy. We must not pollute the land.

We need to use the land and its resources because there are so many people in the world. Everyone needs food and clothes.

Many of the things we wear, use and eat are man-made in factories using non-renewable resources. They need lots of manufacturing and create pollution.

FRAGILE

Sheep are very important because they produce both wool for clothes and meat for food. This helps many people in the world.

Wool is . . .

- **Biodegradable** - it will break down and go back to the soil - unlike plastic.
- **Renewable** - we can produce more of it, unlike oil which is a fossil fuel.
- **Recyclable** - it can be used over and over again.

As well as these things it's good to wear, so wool is well worth producing!

Even though wool is a natural product, having a sheep farm does have an effect on the environment. Farmers must make sure that the land is kept in a healthy state.

Wool is an environmentally friendly product.

Caring for the land

Soil needs nutrients (goodness) in it. Worms and micro-organisms keep it healthy. Australian soils naturally lack phosphorus which all plants use to grow, so it must be added. Farmers use fertilisers to improve the quality of the soil.

Pasture is another name for grass. In many areas of Australia farmers have planted legumes (a special sort of grass) such as clover. Legumes are really good for the soil because they put nitrogen into it. Legumes have enabled a much larger area of Australia to be used

To care for the environment farmers must look at both the land and the sheep that are put on the land.

for sheep farming. Legumes can make the soil acidic which is not good, so to solve this problem the farmer may need to add lime.

Water must be pure. If extra

chemicals get into it the water can harm other animals, plants and people. There have been difficulties with some chemicals getting into the rivers and causing contamination. Some fertilisers have led to the growth of blue/green algae which is a problem in rivers. If the farmer uses chemicals carefully this will not happen.

Trees help stop soil erosion, they help prevent the land getting salty, they give wildlife a place to live, they provide timber for use on the farm and they give shade and shelter to the sheep. Trees are being planted to replace those that were cleared. They are often planted in rows as windbreaks. This stops the wind whistling though the paddocks and is especially helpful for young lambs and for shorn sheep.

Sheep management is also an important part of caring for the environment. Putting too many sheep on a farm (overstocking) or leaving the sheep in a paddock for too long can mean too much grass is eaten and this will lead to soil erosion as there is not enough grass left to hold the soil in place.

Landcare Groups

The Australian government has made the 10 years from 1990-1999 the "Decade of Landcare" and people around Australia have started Landcare groups in their own areas so they can care for their land.

These groups are working really well because it is not the government, but the people living on the land who are deciding for themselves what the problems are and how to fix them. The government will give them some money to help with things like tree planting and stopping soil erosion.

The slogan 'Think global, act local' means that we are aiming to make the whole world a better place to live in. People should work towards this by caring for the environment in their own small community.

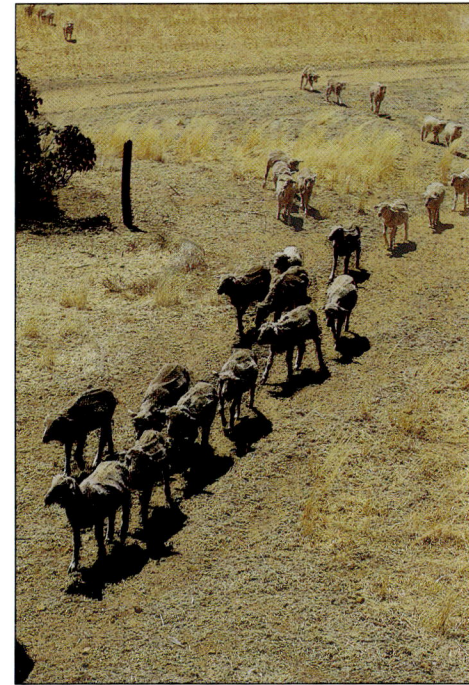

Sheep like to play "follow the leader" when they walk and they often seem to use the same path over again, making tracks. This can cause soil erosion, especially in a creek bed. But the problem is solved by putting a log or a rock across the path — Next time they'll walk a different way.

Using chemicals on the sheep

It would be good if sheep were always healthy and farmers didn't need to use chemicals on them. For this reason, and because no one likes to see sick animals, farmers try to stop the sheep getting pests or diseases wherever possible.

Prevention is better than cure. An example of this is what is being done to stop sheep getting fly struck. Blowfly strike is one of the biggest problems and no one wants to see sheep suffering from an infection caused by maggots.

- The main way to stop this is the operation, called mulesing, which lambs are given when their tails are taken off. This keeps the sheep's bottom much cleaner and it has meant a lot less sheep now get fly struck.
- The CSIRO has developed a vaccine (injection) to stop the sheep getting fleece rot. When a sheep gets fleece rot its skin is wet and infected and the sheep is likely to get fly struck.
- Scientists are also trying to develop a sheep that is resistant to fly strike (it won't get struck).
- Some farmers are now using "bait bins". Bins, painted yellow to attract the flies, are filled with bait and a poison to kill the flies.

However, no matter how hard farmers try, sheep, like people, will get sick. They need medicines or

This is what maggots can do to a sheep. Blowfly strike is a big problem. No one wants to see a maggotty sheep. Yuk!

chemical treatments to help them get better.

As scientists have learnt more about how chemicals can harm the environment (as well as help the sheep) they have continued to improve the treatments so hopefully the chemicals won't have a negative effect on either the sheep, the wool, people who use the products, or our environment.

The chemicals are very carefully screened before they can be used. In fact only one in every 10,000 chemicals ends up being registered for use as a pesticide or animal health drug. It usually takes 10 years from the time it is first tested until the chemical is allowed to be used by the farmers.

Today chemicals are more environmentally safe than ever before. Australia has banned the use of two different types of chemicals because they were found to be bad for the environment. These are organo-chlorines and arsenic.

It is now possible to get chemicals that are:
- Biodegradable - they decompose (break down) after they have killed the pests.
- Species specific - they kill only the one pest (like maggots) and no other insects.
- Safe to use - they are not toxic so they won't harm people (eg. they don't smell so won't give the farmer a headache).

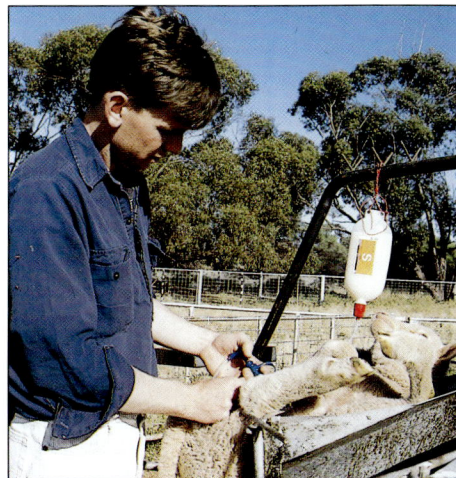

Even though chemicals are safer than ever before, they must still be used with care. Here are some tips farmers follow for the safe use of chemicals.

1. Follow the instructions exactly.

2. Wear clothes that protect you from the chemical like rubber gloves.

3. Keep the chemical in a safe place.

4. Buy only the amount needed.

5. Wash empty drums three times.

6. Don't let any chemicals get into waterways - ie. rivers.

7. Any chemical that is left over must have water added to it to make it weaker and then be poured into a deep pit.

8. Don't use any chemicals just before the sheep are killed for meat or their wool is sold.

Chemicals in the wool

While the chemicals used on sheep to kill parasites do a good job it is important to make sure they don't stay in the wool after it is processed. Chemicals left in the wool are called chemical residues. The consumer (that's you) wants to know that the woollen clothes he or she buys are chemical free and are safe and healthy to wear.

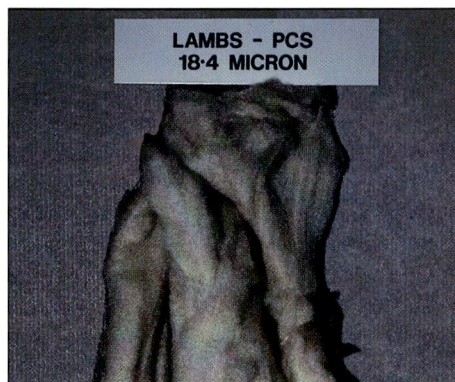

LAMBS - PCS
18·4 MICRON

When the wool is scoured (cleaned) any chemicals still in the wool come out in the wool grease. The cleaned wool becomes free from chemicals but they remain in the wool grease and in the waste water.

Australia wants to be able to sell wool to the world that is environmentally safe so it would be best if there were no chemicals left in the wool at all. The Australian

Tongue twister:
We wondered whether wise wethers wandered in wet weather?

Wool Testing Authority (AWTA) tests the greasy wool before it is sold to check the levels of chemical residues. We were one of the first countries in the world to test to make sure no farmers were using the banned chemicals.

Even though the chemicals used today are safer for our environment than ever before, they can still remain in the wool especially if they were put on the sheep just before shearing and haven't had time to break down. It is possible that one day a withholding period will be introduced - that is a rule to say the farmer can't use the chemicals on the wool close to shearing time.

The scouring process
Wool by-products

Greasy wool on
the sheep.

The shorn wool is washed to remove the dirt.
This is called the scouring process.

Clean wool - chemical free and safe
to wear.

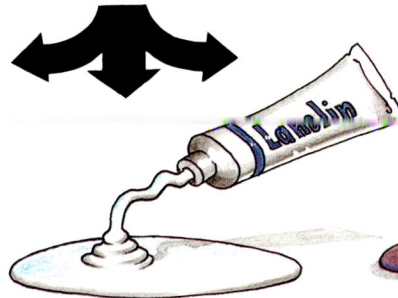

Lanolin comes from the wool grease
and is used by mothers and babies on
their skin. The CSIRO has invented
a process to remove all chemicals
from lanolin.

Dirty water - called waste water
(contains chemicals).
It must be treated very carefully. If it
gets poured into a river it can kill the
fish and other wildlife.

The weather

Just as we can have an effect on the environment with the way we treat it, the environment can affect us. The weather is part of the environment and everything that happens on a farm depends on the weather. In the city the weather is not so important, it's annoying when it doesn't stop raining for days but it doesn't *really* affect your life.

When you live on a farm it does. If there is a **drought** then the dams start to dry up and so do the tanks at the house. Everyone has to be very careful with the water. The children have to use the same bath water, you aren't allowed to flush the toilet when you do a wee and you never leave the tap running when you clean your teeth.

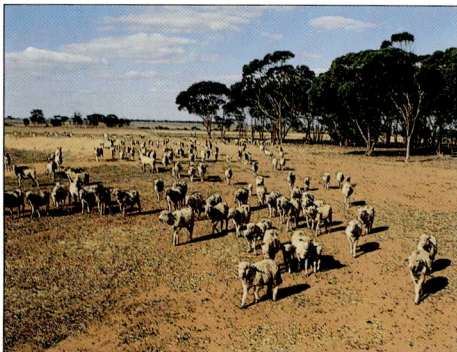

Sometimes, if the drought is very bad, the farmer will have to sell the sheep or shoot them because it's too cruel to see them dying of thirst and hunger.

Floods can be just as awful. The sheep get drowned or stuck in the mud and can die because they can't get out.

Bushfires are a scary part of living on a farm in Australia. Every summer, when it's very hot and the

grass is very dry, the farmers worry about fires. They know if it is a hot, windy day a bushfire can destroy a farm very quickly, burning all the paddocks, the fences, the sheep and the house. It is very important you never do anything that might start a fire.

But even in years when there isn't a flood, bushfire or drought the sheep farmer still depends on

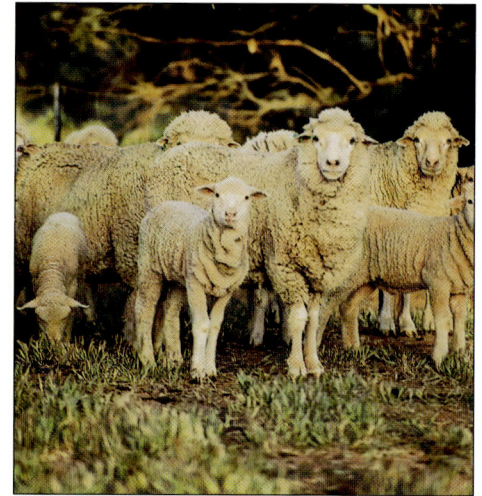

the weather. Everything, from when the ewes have their lambs to when the shearing is done is planned because of the weather. These things change from place to place because the weather is different everywhere.

Of course the weather will also change on each farm from year to

Never have barbeques outside when there is a total fire ban!

The Environment

year and the farmer must do things that weren't done the year before. A hot, wet summer may lead to an outbreak of blowfly strike and the sheep will have to be jetted once or twice whereas in a cool, dry summer it may not be such a problem.

The way the farmer must change plans according to the weather can be compared with some of the things you do. You may usually be able to swim in November but children who live elsewhere may not. However, you wouldn't go swimming just because it was November if the weather was still very cold.

Sheep farming is a seasonal occupation and activities are planned because of the weather. Each farm will be slightly different. It does not matter when the activities happen but rather what the activities are.

The most important thing to understand about sheep farming is the way the source, the farmer, the product, the consumer and the environment all interact. Each depends on the others for the continual production of high quality wool.

INDEX